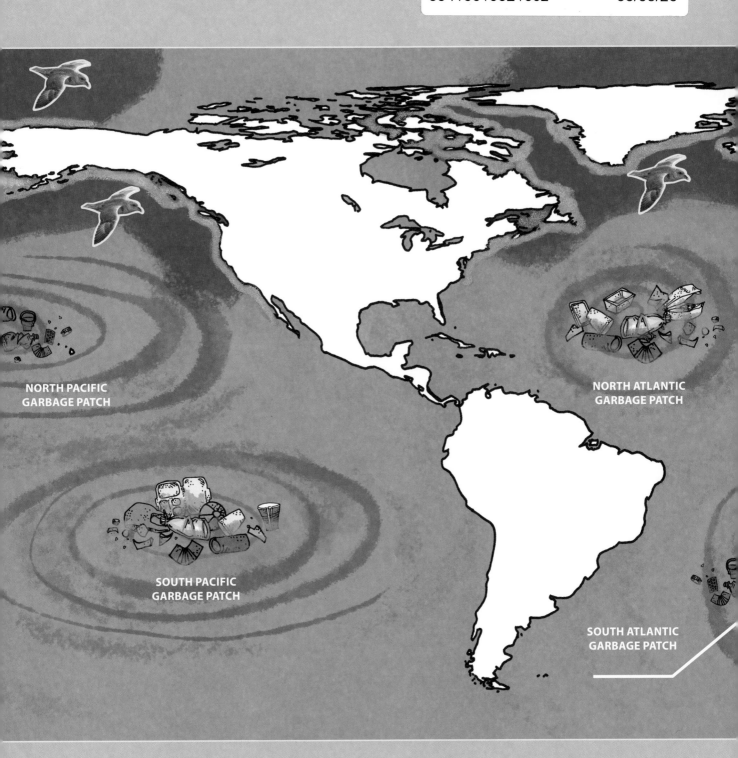

PLASTIC SEA

A Bird's-eye View

ISBN: 978-1-943645-50-3

10 9 8 7 6 5 4 3 2 1

Printed in the United States of America

CPSIA tracking label information
Production Location: CG Book Printers
North Mankato, Minnesota
Production Date: February 2020
Cohort: Batch No. 294302

Image credits
Shutterstock photos: floating trash pp. 14-15; sand toys p. 16; orange
drink bottles p. 18; fishing net p. 21; toothbrush and paint can p. 23;
ghost net pp 24-25; Northern Gannet with fishing net p. 27; toy on
the beach pp. 30-31; globe p. 32; tire p. 37; seabirds and fishing boat
pp. 38-39; decomposed golf ball p. 41; plastic bottles pp. 42-43; hands
with plastic bits p. 45; ball of plastic garbage p. 54; hands picking up
plastic trash p. 55; compressed plastic waste p. 61. Espen Bergersen:
fulmar reflected p. 4; Susanne Kühn: fulmar with food p. 5; Georg
Bangjord: fulmars near boat and net p. 6; Hallvard Strøm: fulmar
with egg p. 7; Dorian Anderson/Macaulay Library: two fulmars p.
7; Odd Harald Selboskar: fulmar and chick p. 8; Annelies Leeuw/
Alamy Stock Photo: spitting fulmar p. 8; Odd Kindberg: two fulmars
p. 9; Jan van Franeker–IMARES: plastic found inside a fulmar,
Sebastien Descamps: flying fulmar p. 10; Ilana Nimz: Brown Noddy
using plastic debris on nest p. 11; Shutterstock/Paisan Changhirun:
facts garbage cans on pp. 12, 14, 22, 45; Susanne Kühn: fulmar eats
plastic p. 12; Chris Jordan: plastic inside a dead albatross p. 13; Alice
Trevail: Lego p. 17; Getty Images/Stockbyte: dolphin, and Ewan
Edwards: entangled seal p. 26; Troy Mayne: turtle eating plastic bag
and D. K. Coughran: entangled whale p. 28; Missouri Department
of Conservation: turtle with plastic rings, and Bo Eide: Northern
Gannet with chicks p. 29; Mélanie Chamorel: chair on the seafloor,
and DPAW Western Australia: tire underwater p. 33; Steve White/
U.S.Navy/Reuters/NTB Scanpix: plastic trash from an airplane
window and Alexander Todd/U.S. Navy/Reuters/NTB Scanpix:
tsunami wreckage p. 34; Baltimore Trash Wheel p. 36; Geir Wing
Gabrielsen: seabirds grazing p. 35; Ida Beathe Øverjordet and Dag
Altin: plankton p. 40; Bo Eide: girl cleaning beach p. 44; Bahamas
Plastic Movement: pp. 46, 47, 51, and 53; Jeon Heon-Kyun/EPA/NTB
Scanpix: Boyan Slat p. 49; Pedro Armestre: plastic in fishing nets
p. 52; Hallvard Strøm: fulmar couple p. 57; Steve Heinl/Macaulay
Library: fulmars nesting p. 58-59; Stein Ø. Nilsen: flying fulmar
p. 62; Kirsti Blom: beach background and Johanna Blom and Ingrid
Gabrielsen: author photos p. 63; Alex Lamoreaux/Macaulay Library:
flying fulmar, jacket and p. 64. Rivers graph p. 37 based on "Export of
Plastic Debris by Rivers into the Sea," by Christian Schmidt et al., in
Environmental Science & Technology, Vol. 51, No. 21; November 7, 2017.

Kirsti Blom received support from the Nonfiction Literary Fund to
write the book. The Norwegian Polar Institute, The Fram Centre,
and the Svalbard Environmental Protection Fund supported its
publication in Norway.

The **Cornell** Lab
Publishing Group

An imprint of WunderMill, Inc.
120A North Salem Street
Apex, NC 27502

WunderMillBooks.com

PLASTIC SEA

A Bird's-eye View

KIRSTI BLOM AND GEIR WING GABRIELSEN

Translated by Helle Valborg Goldman

The**Cornell**Lab Publishing Group

A SEABIRD'S SEARCH

Riding the ocean wind, a Northern Fulmar glides just above the waves. He needs only a few beats of his wings as he steers between the wave crests. All the while, he scans the surface of the water for food. He's a seabird adapted for survival on the open ocean.

The fulmar spots something gleaming on the sea's dark mirror. Is it a crunchy crustacean or a silvery squid? With his powerful beak, the bird snaps up his prey and gulps it down. Then he's already on the lookout for more marine creatures, or their eggs, to fill his stomach.

A COLORFUL CATCH

The fulmar has a keen sense of smell. He catches the scent of fish from a fishing boat and flies toward it. Someone on the boat is flinging fish waste into the water. Soon, the fulmar and a whole flock of seabirds are pouncing on fish remains in the wake behind the boat.

Some of today's catch is extra colorful. Green and yellow morsels slide down the Northern Fulmar's throat, but what he doesn't know is that with the fish pieces, he's also just swallowed floating plastic garbage.

The Northern Fulmar's catch is more multicolored today than in decades past. That's because humans are making more plastic than ever before, especially disposable products that get used once and tossed away. These plastic objects are part of our daily lives and often offer convenience, but too much plastic has become ocean trash, causing great harm to the seabirds that eat it.

A FULMAR FAMILY

Over the ocean, Northern Fulmars are magnificent and agile fliers. On land, they're clumsy and barely able to walk. They often make their simple nests on cliffs so they can launch themselves straight into the air.

Northern Fulmars can live more than 50 years, about twice as long as a gull. Every year in the spring, a mated fulmar pair meets at the same nest.

The female lays her first egg when she's 8–10 years old. The fulmar parents take turns sitting on the egg, keeping it warm and dry for about seven weeks.

A Northern Fulmar couple shares a nest site.

RAISING A FULMAR CHICK

Once the chick hatches, the parents feed it by spitting up food they have eaten. The chick scoops up the regurgitated food from the parents' mouths. Sadly, parents feed their chick tiny bits of plastic too. Because of this, the young ball of downy feathers may begin life with trash inside its body.

After two weeks, the parents can leave the chick alone during their long flights to find food.

The growing chick knows how to defend itself from predators such as Glaucous Gulls and Great Black-backed Gulls. Like its parents, the chick spits a stinking oil at predatory birds—up to 6 feet (1.8 meters) away!

When predators' feathers get matted with fulmar oil, they will not repel water. A predator with oiled feathers will die of cold and hunger, so they know to keep their distance. Fulmar oil is an amazing defense for young birds.

The Northern Fulmar soars over the vast ocean, as he has for many seasons since he first hatched on a cliff ledge. With his mate, he has raised more than 20 young fulmars on the same nest. If conditions are good, the female fulmar lays one white egg to produce a single chick. Within a couple months, the chick fledges: it grows flight feathers to replace downy feathers and flies away.

Each winter, the parents separate. The female fulmar heads south to Nova Scotia, while the male stays in Newfoundland. Through raging winter storms, they hunker alone on cliff ledges for up to two weeks at a stretch, not moving or feeding, just waiting for the weather to break. Neither bird will starve—a store of rich oil in their bodies keeps them alive. The oil comes from the fish, crustaceans, and squids they eat. Each spring, the male and female reunite at their nest to lay an egg and raise a new chick, if the sea provides enough food.

One summer, the Northern Fulmar parents can barely feed their chick because the female is too weak to fly away and bring back food. Laying her egg, keeping the egg warm till it hatches, and then keeping the chick fed seem to be too much for her. Is she sick?

A PROBLEM WITH PLASTIC

The next spring, the female does not return, and the male fulmar is alone. He doesn't know that his mate died because her stomach was filled with plastic. Scientists find her body washed up on the shore and discover the plastic when they examine her.

Plastic bits found inside a dead Northern Fulmar.

On Kure Atoll, a Brown Noddy and chick sit on a nest of plastic debris.

Scientists already know that about 90% of Northern Fulmars have plastic in their stomachs. Northern Fulmars aren't the only seabirds suffering from encounters with plastic in the ocean. Ocean plastic harms some other kinds of seabirds. Half of all seabird species pluck food from the ocean surface or just below, like Northern Fulmars do.

South of the equator, albatrosses eat a lot of floating ocean plastic. And on islands more than 1,240 miles [1996 kilometers] from any human population, female albatrosses now lay eggs among plastic lighters, detergent bottles, hair brushes, fishing net scraps, and polystyrene food containers that have washed ashore.

DID YOU KNOW?

THE WORLD MAKES 350 MILLION TONS OF PLASTIC EVERY YEAR.

A BELLY FULL OF PLASTIC

Why do seabirds eat floating plastic in the ocean? It looks like the food that they eat. It also smells like it because as the plastic floats, it becomes coated with algae and bacteria from the ocean. Eating even a few tiny plastic fragments causes a bird distress.

However, it isn't just bits of plastic that are big enough for us to see that end up in a seabird's stomach. When they are far from fresh water, Northern Fulmars and other seabirds drink salty ocean water when they are thirsty because they have a special salt gland at the base of their bill that gets rid of the extra salt. Unfortunately, there is no way to get rid of the microplastics in the seawater they drink, or in the food they eat.

Floating plastic can look, smell, and taste like the Northern Fulmar's natural food.

A Northern Fulmar feels full when it swallows plastic, but the plastic has no nutrients, so the birds become malnourished. Plastic takes two to three months to pass out of birds' bodies as poop, but some of the plastic gets stuck in the stomach or intestines and never makes it out.

Plastic pieces also injure a seabird's internal organs, reducing its appetite and causing pain and even death. Many fulmars are suffering. People now see fewer flocks of fulmars riding the ocean whitecaps and following fishing boats.

This is what was found inside a dead albatross.

Northern Fulmars are a "bioindicator species." Scientists use Northern Fulmars as a measuring stick for how much plastic is floating on the ocean. The more fulmars that are found with a stomach full of plastic, the more plastic scientists know is in the sea. The birds can't speak directly to us, but their fate is a warning to us that there's too much plastic waste in the ocean.

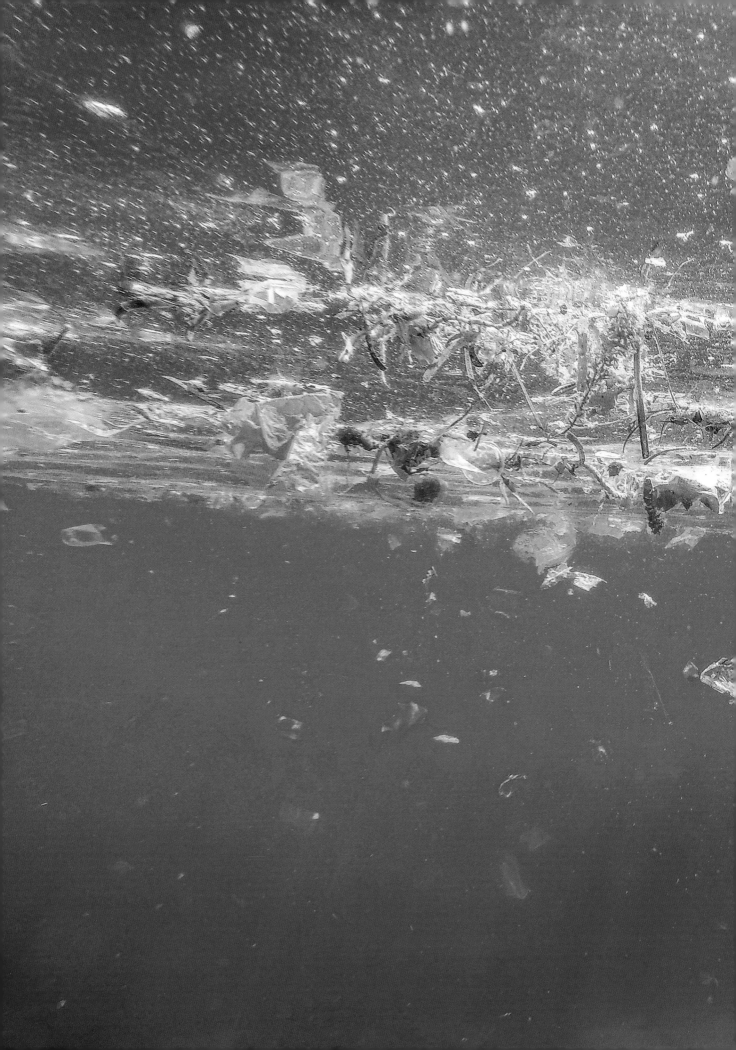

DID YOU KNOW?

AROUND THE WORLD, MORE THAN A MILLION PLASTIC BOTTLES ARE SOLD EVERY MINUTE.

THE AGE OF PLASTIC

The word "plastic" comes from the Greek word plastikos meaning "able to be molded." Plastic is made from oil.

It is useful and convenient because machines can shape it into all kinds of objects like computers, sports gear, shoes, telephones, eating utensils, clothing, food packaging, toys, kitchen equipment, polystyrene boxes, bottles, cups, and other containers. Plastic can be hard or soft. Some types float, while others sink.

The problem is that we don't keep our plastic products forever. We throw

Discarded plastic toys on the beach.

them out when they break or we don't need them anymore. Despite world news about huge floating garbage patches, and marine animals dying from plastic, humans continue to dump mountains of garbage into the oceans.

In 1997, a storm off England's coast tumbled 5,000,000 Lego® toy pieces from a ship into the ocean. Hard plastic dragons, swords, and black squids are still washing up on land. Despite years of being exposed to storms, sun, and saltwater, many of the toys are intact and can be used. Hard plastic takes much longer to decay than soft plastic. British children still make trips to the beach to look for the toys. Meanwhile, ocean currents spread the millions of toys even farther from where they first fell into the sea.

No one knows where they all are.

BREAKING IT DOWN

Paper, orange peels, apple cores, and other organic matter decompose quickly in the ocean. Plastic takes much longer, and never completely disappears. Light and heat break plastic down, but in the cold, dark sea, plastic breaks down much more slowly.

A plastic grocery bag may be used for an hour, but it takes 10-20 years to disintegrate; polystyrene cups take 50 years; disposable diapers or plastic bottles take 450 years; fishing lines take 600 years!

Plastic bottles are a huge source of plastic waste.

HOW LONG UNTIL IT'S GONE?

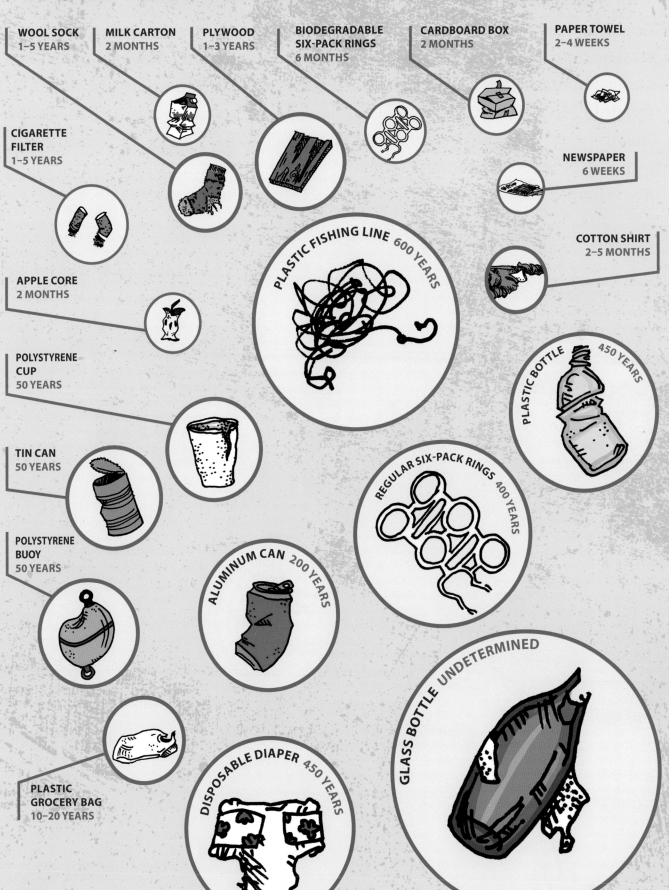

WOOL SOCK
1–5 YEARS

MILK CARTON
2 MONTHS

PLYWOOD
1–3 YEARS

BIODEGRADABLE SIX-PACK RINGS
6 MONTHS

CARDBOARD BOX
2 MONTHS

PAPER TOWEL
2–4 WEEKS

CIGARETTE FILTER
1–5 YEARS

NEWSPAPER
6 WEEKS

APPLE CORE
2 MONTHS

COTTON SHIRT
2–5 MONTHS

POLYSTYRENE CUP
50 YEARS

PLASTIC FISHING LINE 600 YEARS

PLASTIC BOTTLE 450 YEARS

TIN CAN
50 YEARS

REGULAR SIX-PACK RINGS 400 YEARS

POLYSTYRENE BUOY
50 YEARS

ALUMINUM CAN 200 YEARS

GLASS BOTTLE UNDETERMINED

PLASTIC GROCERY BAG
10–20 YEARS

DISPOSABLE DIAPER 450 YEARS

PLASTIC TRASH COMES IN ALL SIZES

Megaplastics are the largest pieces and include drifting fishing nets, plastic sheets, and other objects just over 1 yard (1 meter) or larger. **Macroplastics** are next, with pieces just over 3/16 inches (5 millimeters) to just over 1 yard (1 meter). **Microplastics** are barely visible, ranging from less than 3/16 inches to 1 micrometer* (to give you an idea of how small a micrometer is, the average human hair is 100 micrometers thick). Plastic never vanishes—it just crumbles into **nanoplastics**, the smallest pieces visible only under a microscope.

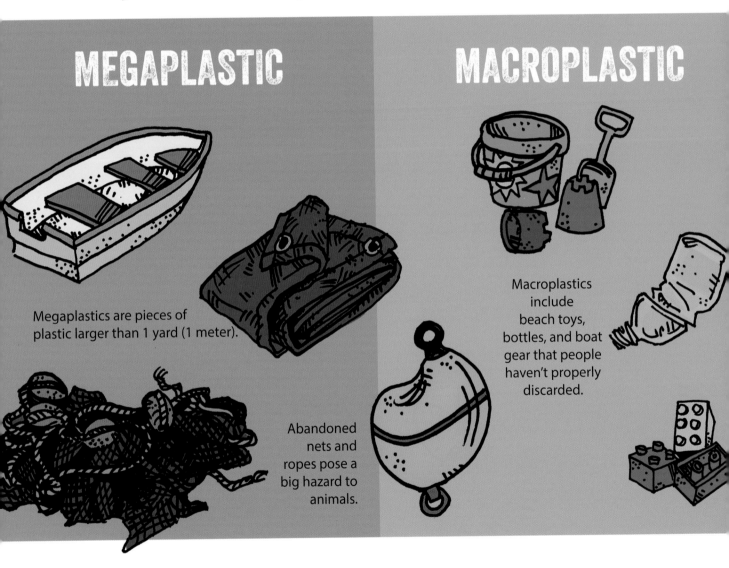

MEGAPLASTIC

Megaplastics are pieces of plastic larger than 1 yard (1 meter).

Abandoned nets and ropes pose a big hazard to animals.

MACROPLASTIC

Macroplastics include beach toys, bottles, and boat gear that people haven't properly discarded.

You

Dog

Ant

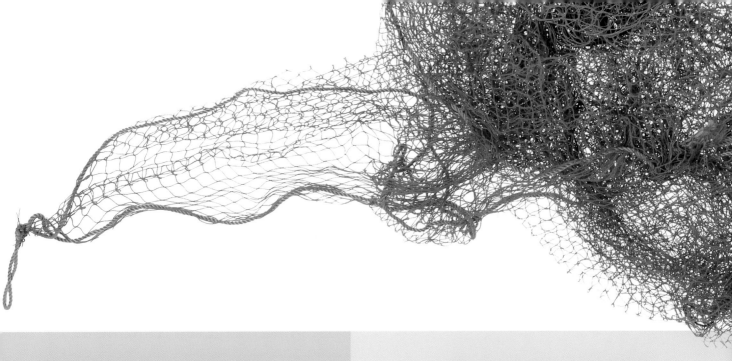

MICROPLASTIC

NANOPLASTIC

In the U.S.A. alone, tires shed 1.8 million tons of microplastic particles each year. We don't know how much of this ends up in the ocean.

Some cosmetics contain microplastics.

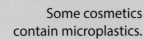

Microplastics from paint flow in streams or rivers to the ocean.

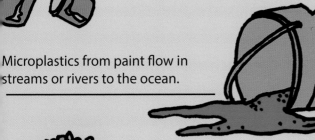

 Mite

 Bacteria

 Virus

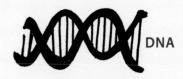 DNA

*1 micrometer (μm) is the same as 0.001 millimeter

DID YOU KNOW?

WASTEWATER FROM WASHING MACHINES IS A SOURCE OF OCEAN PLASTIC.

TINY PLASTICS— HUGE POLLUTANT

Much of the plastic waste in the ocean is in very small pieces (the microplastics and nanoplastics you just read about). In our everyday lives, we may be adding microplastics to the ocean without even realizing it.

For many years, toothpastes, lotions, detergents, shower gels, shaving foams, and facial scrubs had plastic microbeads added to whiten our teeth and add a silky texture to lotions.

Fleece jackets and all kinds of clothing made from polyester, acrylic, and nylon contain tiny plastic fibers that are shed in the washing machine. These countless fibers drain into pipes that carry dirty water away.

Microplastics are added to paint and other products for street painting and to keep houses and boats in good condition. People may carelessly rinse their brushes onto the ground or into storm drains, where the microplastics eventually flow to the ocean.

Wastewater treatment plants filter the water, but plastic microbeads and fibers are too small to be trapped and are ultimately washed out to the sea.

Thankfully, microbeads in cosmetics, toothpaste, and paint have been banned in many countries, and there is a strong international movement toward universal bans of microplastics.

How does microplastic move from our shores all the way to the Arctic and the Antarctic Oceans? It travels to the ocean in rivers and through drain pipes. In the ocean, some of the microplastic is eaten by small filter-feeding animals like krill. Ocean currents carry the tiny animals and microplastic to the open ocean where larger fish, marine mammals, and seabirds eat the krill and the microplastic. And when larger fish and mammals move from coastal waters to the deep ocean, they might take some plastic with them inside their bellies.

MANY ANIMALS SUFFER

Abandoned fishing nets, called "ghost nets," are also made of plastic. They drift about in oceans all over the world and are extremely harmful to marine life, including coral reefs. Collecting them is part of the global effort to clean up our oceans.

This dolphin died after being caught in a ghost net.

Even huge whales can lose their lives to drifting ghost nets, fishing lines, and the plastic they eat. Whales have other problems with ocean plastic. Scientists are finding more and more whales washed up on beaches with plastic in their stomachs. In 2019, a dead Cuvier's beaked whale on a beach in the Philippines had 88 pounds (40 kilograms) of plastic bags, rice sacks, and other objects in its stomach. The whale's digestive juices couldn't break down the plastic—there was so much plastic that there was no space for actual food. In a recent study, scientists found microplastics in the digestive tract of every marine animal they examined.

Plastic kills about 100,000 seals every year.

More than 800 marine species are affected by plastic pollution. Sea turtles gulp down floating plastic shopping bags which get stuck in the turtles' throats or intestines.

Seals, dolphins, seabirds, and penguins become tangled in ropes and fishing lines and may drown. If these animals don't drown, fishing lines can slice through their skin and can damage birds' wings and feathers.

Plastic bags mimic ocean jellies or squids and smell like food.

This whale was set free!

This turtle was rescued and survived!

How do plastic bags end up in the ocean where sea turtles think they are food? One way is that the wind picks up empty plastic bags from inland areas and carries them to streams and rivers flowing to the sea.

A Northern Gannet holds a piece of abandoned fishing net in its beak.

GARBAGE GOES GLOBAL

How a nation handles its garbage affects other nations. In the ocean, garbage doesn't stop at national borders or coastlines—it goes global with ocean currents.

In 2014, scientists estimated there were more than five trillion plastic pieces in the sea. Recently, scientists studying the flow of plastic from riverbeds to the ocean have concluded that this estimate is probably far short of the actual number.

Individuals in wealthy countries typically produce more garbage than those in developing countries, and countries with

In the world's oceans, 94% of the plastic lies at the bottom of the sea, 5% washes up on beaches, and 1% is floating on the surface.

more people often throw away more plastic than countries with fewer people. Even so, small and developing countries may not have enough resources to clean up their trash, and that means more ocean plastic is contributed per person in these countries than in larger or more developed countries. So the

amount of trash per person and where that trash ends up changes from country to country.

Beyond the garbage we can see on ocean surfaces, scientists think the largest portion of ocean plastic pollution actually sinks to the seafloor. There, plastic settles into muddy sediment, catches on plants and stones, or sits in deep underwater canyons. The ocean bottom is much darker and colder, and the water has less oxygen than the ocean surface. Plastic in the deep ocean takes an even longer time to disintegrate than plastic on the ocean's surface.

THE GREAT OCEAN GARBAGE PATCHES

The Great Pacific Garbage Patch is a broad area between Japan and the United States where ocean currents spin in a "gyre," a giant circular current on the ocean's surface. Marine debris accumulates in a soup of plastic confetti. The size of the plastic debris in the gyres varies from quite large to microscopic and is distributed from the ocean's surface to the ocean deep.

In 2011, a 9.0 earthquake near Japan made the patches bigger. The quake triggered a colossal wave—a tsunami—that tore across the Japanese landscape. As the wave pulled back from the land, the water dragged houses, boats, factories, and cars out to sea. The Earth's rotation, major wind patterns, and ocean currents then mixed the earthquake debris with floating plastic bottles, bottle caps, lighters, toothbrushes, fishing nets, toys, soccer balls, boats, canoes, sandals, balloons, pipes, tires, hair brushes, fleece jackets, plastic straws, and other trash.

Waste from the tsunami floating in the ocean.

Four other garbage whirlpools have developed: near Cuba, between Australia and South America, between Africa and Australia, and between Africa and South America. If ocean garbage keeps increasing, a huge patch could also appear in other places, like the Barents Sea, north of Norway.

The Barents Sea is a springtime feeding ground for 15 million seabirds that fatten up on fish, amphipods, and krill before they head to the Arctic coast to lay eggs and raise their young. Those seabirds would be in great danger should that whirlpool develop.

Plastic trash seen from an airplane window.

RIVERS TO THE SEA

How does all this plastic garbage end up in the ocean? Where does it come from? The garbage in the ocean isn't just from people leaving plastic toys on the beach. Rivers can transport pollutants long distances and are a huge contributor to ocean plastic pollution.

One big source of plastic pollution is from car tires that shed countless particles from wear and tear. When it rains and snow melts, these particles run into streams that flow to rivers and the sea.

Some cities are starting to address the problem of rivers carrying plastic to the ocean. The Trash Wheel Project in Baltimore, Maryland, removes rubbish from Baltimore's Inner Harbor before it reaches the open ocean. The wheel once collected 38,000 pounds (17,200 kilograms) in a single day!

The garbage collected in Baltimore's Inner Harbor is used to make electricity.

THE TOP 12 RIVERS THAT CARRY PLASTIC TO THE SEA

CONTINENTS / RIVERS TO SEAS

Mekong River → South China Sea
Asia — **1.9 million**

Niger River → Gulf of Guinea
Africa — **2.0 million**

Amur River → Sea of Okhotsk
Asia — **2.1 million**

Pearl River → South China Sea
Asia — **2.5 million**

Meghna, Brahmaputra, and Ganges Rivers → Bay of Bengal
Asia — **3.0 million**

Nile River → Mediterranean Sea
Africa — **3.3 million**

Hai He River → Yellow Sea
Asia — **3.4 million**

Yellow River → Yellow Sea
Asia — **4.1 million**

Indus River → Arabian Sea
Asia — **4.8 million**

Yangtze River → Yellow Sea
Asia — **16.9 million**

MISMANAGED PLASTIC WASTE (TONS/YEAR)

THESE 12 RIVERS TOGETHER CARRY ABOUT 90% OF THE PLASTIC THAT REACHES THE OCEAN!

A TOXIC FEAST

Why is plastic so deadly to birds and other sea animals? Ecotoxins, like pesticides and industrial pollutants, stick to plastic like a coating. Pesticides get into the ocean the same way some microplastics do—washed from the land by rain, into streams and rivers that open into the sea. When animals eat the plastic, the harmful chemicals get inside their bodies.

The smaller the plastic, the higher the concentration of ecotoxins. As plastic breaks down, it releases these chemicals into ocean water. Ecotoxins in seawater make their way into the marine food web. Tiny crustaceans, such as krill and other floating plankton, absorb ecotoxins from seawater, or eat tiny pieces of coated plastic, accumulating even more poisons inside their bodies.

Many fish species eat mainly zooplankton. These tiny animals reproduce in spring, and fish gorge on this food to gain energy for the beginning of the breeding season. Plankton can be so small you can't see them without a microscope, or they can be as large as krill or jellies, which are actually plankton too. But no matter how small or large they are, all plankton may have ecotoxins from polluted sea water. When fish eat plankton as their main food, the poisons build up in the fish. Then seals, whales, Northern Fulmars, and other seabirds feast on poisoned fish.

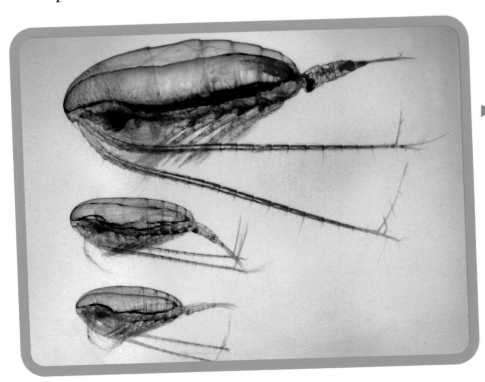

Plankton is essential food for many fish species.

When a seabird eats a lot of contaminated fish, ecotoxins become more concentrated in the bird's liver and fat. With the hard work of egg laying, the fat in the mother bird breaks down to give the bird more energy. Then the poisons enter her bloodstream, and she gets sicker and weaker. She struggles to fly and bring back enough food for her chicks. She may become sick and die, and then her chick might starve.

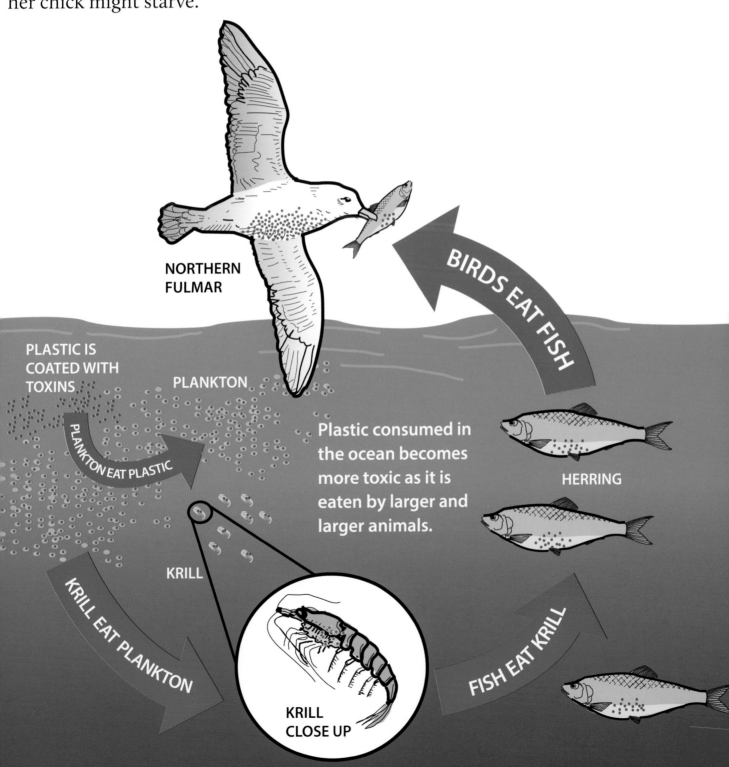

NORTHERN FULMAR

BIRDS EAT FISH

PLASTIC IS COATED WITH TOXINS

PLANKTON

PLANKTON EAT PLASTIC

Plastic consumed in the ocean becomes more toxic as it is eaten by larger and larger animals.

HERRING

KRILL

KRILL EAT PLANKTON

FISH EAT KRILL

KRILL CLOSE UP

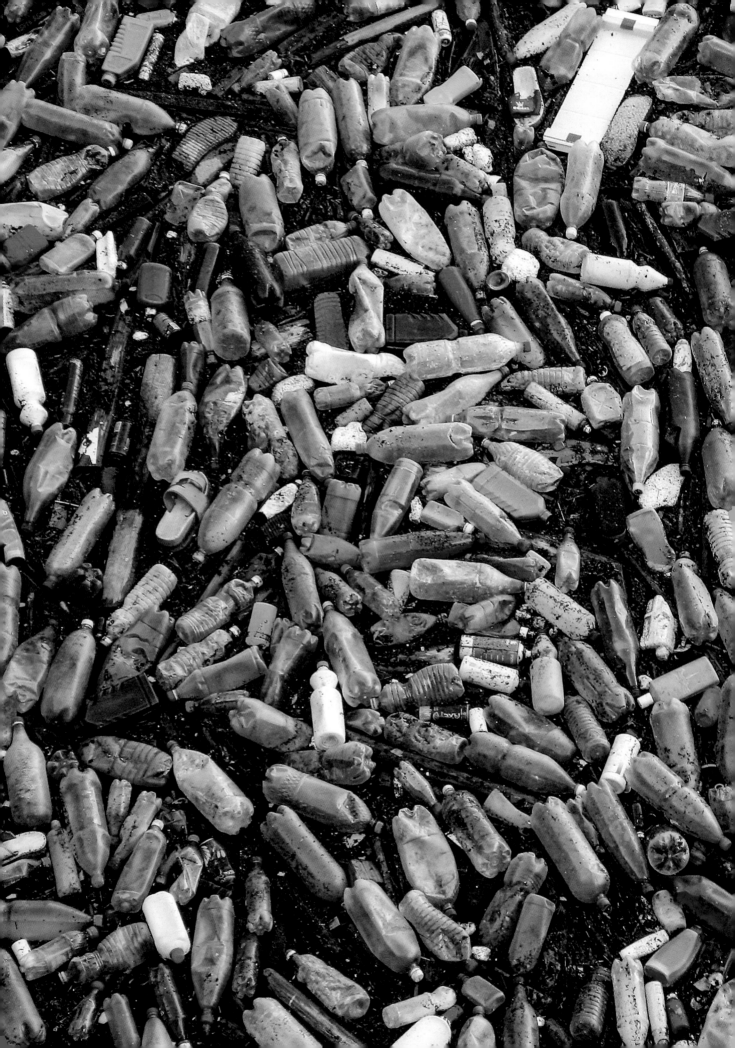

YOU CAN HELP!

Plastic pollution is a BIG problem, but young environmentalists all over the world are proving that you don't have to be an adult to make a difference. From the Netherlands to the Bahamas, and here in the United States, young people are attacking the problem of plastics through thoughtful planning and scientific study, creative problem-solving, and community organization.

DID YOU KNOW?

ONLY 9% OF PLASTIC WASTE IS ACTUALLY RECYCLED.

YOUNG OCEAN HEROES

Kristal Ambrose, an environmental educator in the Bahamas, founded the Bahamas Plastic Movement after seeing the harmful effects of plastic pollution on her home island of Eleuthera. The Bahamas are not big enough for large-scale recycling, so her group works with locals to combat plastic pollution on their islands through other actions, like refusing plastic straws and talking to government officials about anti-plastics laws.

Kristal and her students also visit their local beach to collect data on the plastic there. This helps them better understand where the plastic is coming from and how to prevent further pollution. In 2018, Kristal and her students successfully engaged the Bahamian government in working toward a countrywide ban on single-use plastics, polystyrene, and balloon releases by 2020.

Students in the Bahamas Plastic Movement gather data about plastic pollution by collecting and examining ocean debris. They also clean up plastic trash at local beaches.

PASSION PUT INTO ACTION

Just like Kristal Ambrose and the Bahamas Plastics Movement, the Ocean Heroes Bootcamp in Canada (conceived by Lonely Whale and the Captain Planet Foundation, and supported by Point Break Foundation) offers workshops for young leaders to educate, organize, and activate today's youth in the fight against plastic pollution.

Founded in 2018, the camp teaches children and teens to create their own anti-plastics campaigns over three days of campaign development, discussions on plastics-related topics, and grassroots organization instruction. Campers are given the tools and support to develop successful anti-plastics campaigns when they return home, ready to bring the fight against plastic pollution to their own communities.

Sometimes, anti-plastics campaigns can start with family and friends. Alex Weber, a student and free diver in California, works with her father and friends to remove tens of thousands of golf balls from the ocean. Golf balls don't float, so these trained diver-environmentalists must dive to remove them by hand. This kind of volunteer work can't get all the plastic out of the ocean, but every bit helps.

In the U.S.A., as many as 300 million golf balls are lost in bodies of water every year.

New technology is playing a part in ocean clean-up efforts. Ideas being considered or tried include giant ocean vacuum cleaners, plastic-eating bacteria, and even burying deep ocean garbage under sand. Sometimes clean-up inventions don't work, but people keep exploring new ways to get it done.

Boyan Slat was just 18 when he founded The Ocean Cleanup, a nonprofit in the Netherlands dedicated to developing anti-plastic technology. Today, Boyan and a growing team of engineers and scientists are hard at work on a clean-up device, known as a passive drifting system, that moves with ocean currents to collect plastic.

If successful, passive drifting systems could decrease the size of ocean gyres of accumulated plastic by half in five years.

"TAKING CARE OF THE WORLD'S MARINE PROBLEMS IS ONE OF THE GREATEST ENVIRONMENTAL CHALLENGES HUMANITY IS FACING TODAY."
—BOYAN SLAT

JOIN THE FIGHT!

No one person is to blame for plastics in the ocean, but each of us has some responsibility. You can't stop plastic pollution all by yourself, but your actions can make a difference.

Young people can play an important role in controlling how much plastic is in the ocean by changing how and when they use plastic at home and at school, and by helping with clean-up efforts.

Shopping for food that is not in plastic containers, using recyclable bags instead of disposable plastic grocery bags, and recycling plastic helps reduce plastic waste.

Every May, children and adults around the world pick up trash on the beach on International Coastal Cleanup Day. Even if you don't live near the ocean, look for water clean-ups in your own community, or clean up trash yourself any day of the year (if accompanied by an adult). The more plastic we pick up on the beach or inland, the more we'll keep it out of the ocean.

Look around your kitchen, bathroom, and bedroom for unnecessary plastic. Ask about recycling and clean-up programs at your school and in your neighborhood.

Every one of us can take steps to help protect the ocean—including you. If nothing is being done, ask a parent or teacher to help you start something!

Cleaning up a beach with your friends can be fun!

YOUR ACTIONS CAN MAKE A DIFFERENCE.

✓ **What can you do TODAY to help reduce plastic waste?**

✓ **What is happening in your community, and how can you participate?**

✓ **What can you do in your own home?**

SOME PROGRESS

No one owns the open ocean—it is without borders. Countries and cities all over the world are taking action to ban and slow down the accumulation of plastic waste, especially targeting single-use plastics (plastic that is used once and thrown away).

Canada is banning all plastic straws, bags, plates, and stir sticks by 2021. The European Union voted to ban the top ten single-use plastic items found on European beaches by 2021 and wants 90% of plastic bottles recycled by 2025.

In Kenya, plastic bags are banned, and if you are caught using one, you must pay a heavy fine. India, the second most populated country after China, will eliminate single-use plastic entirely by 2022. Peru banned single-use plastics from all-natural areas and museums and is phasing out the use of plastic bags over three years.

Some countries are paying fishermen to trawl for trash instead of fish.

The city of San Diego banned polystyrene containers, including polystyrene cups and egg cartons, because they are almost impossible to recycle. The San Francisco International Airport recently banned the sale of all plastic water bottles. Restaurants in Washington, D.C., and Seattle are fined if they give away plastic straws, and there is a global movement to ban plastic straws entirely.

Nations need to fund more research and support inventions that could truly reduce plastic waste in their own countries and worldwide.

THINK GLOBALLY, ACT LOCALLY.

✓ **What ideas can you think of to help get plastic out of the ocean?**

TAKE THE FIRST STEP

Here are some steps you can take to reduce your own plastic waste:

✔ Start by finding out how much plastic you use in a year with this online plastic consumption calculator: www.earthday.org/plastic-calculator

✔ Design your own anti-plastic pledge online with National Geographic's "Planet or Plastic" pledge, and challenge your friends to do the same: www.nationalgeographic.com/environment/plasticpledge

✔ Buy snacks in bulk, instead of individual plastic packages, and carry them in reusable containers.

✔ Visit a recycling center or waste treatment plant and learn more about plastic pollution. Talk to your friends, family, and classmates about what you learned.

Not everything we buy needs plastic packaging.

✓ Help clean up a beach or stream in your community. Pick up trash at school or in your own neighborhood, even if someone else dropped the litter. Invite friends to go with you!

✓ Write to your local, state, or federal elected government officials and tell them you support laws to protect and clean up the ocean.

✓ Take care not to throw plastic and any other trash in the ocean, on beaches or other natural areas, along roadsides, in the schoolyard, on the street, or even in the toilet. This keeps trash—even trash that starts inland—from being blown or carried by streams and rivers to the sea.

✓ Invite an environmental scientist or someone involved in plastic clean-up to speak to your class or school.

✓ Ask your school and local businesses to set up more public recycling bins and stations.

HOMECOMING

It is springtime again. The old Northern Fulmar searches for food along the windy coast, like hundreds of millions of other seabirds. His strong wings carry him over a beach.

Something is going on below. There are people dashing to and fro collecting garbage.

The male Northern Fulmar flies further on, until he reaches his old nesting site. His longtime mate is gone. He wheels in close to the rocky ledge, but a young Northern Fulmar pair has claimed the little shelf on the cliff. One of these new residents might be the old fulmar's own chick—they like to nest where they were hatched.

They cackle harshly to let him know this is their spot now. They'll defend their nest for all they're worth.

With a few stiff flaps of his wings, the old Northern Fulmar soars out over the sea. Night is falling, but that doesn't stop him.

He's not too old to find a new mate and start again. He swoops acrobatically among the whitecaps and snaps up a tempting morsel. This time, luckily, it's a fat little fish that winds up in his stomach.

WORDS TO REMEMBER
FOR ALL YOUNG OCEAN HEROES

adapted

algae

bacteria

ban

bioindicator

cosmetics

crustacean

debris

decay

decompose

disintegrate

earthquake

ecotoxin

environment

environmentalist

equator

gouge

ingest

intact

jelly

macroplastics

malnourished

megaplastics

microbeads

microplastics

nanoplastics

organic

oxygen

pesticides

plankton

pollution

polystyrene

recycle

regurgitate

seabird

sediment

synthetic

technology

toxin

tsunami

waste treatment plant

whirlpool

Kirsti Blom writes prose and fiction books, and is a recognized speaker. Among other projects, she has collaborated with scientists to write Norwegian children's books about walruses (2005), reindeer (2018), Arctic foxes (2003), polar bears (2007), lemmings (2019), Rock Ptarmigans (2009), Barnacle Geese (2015), Snowy Owls (2017), and Arctic seabirds (2011), as well as a book for young people about snow, ice, and the climate (2008).

Geir Wing Gabrielsen is a biologist and section leader on pollutants at the Norwegian Polar Institute in Tromsø. He is a Norwegian representative in the United Nations Environment Programme specializing in marine litter.

The**Cornell**Lab of Ornithology

The Cornell Lab of Ornithology is a world leader in the study, appreciation, and conservation of birds. As with all Cornell Lab Publishing Group books, 35% of the net proceeds from the sale of *Plastic Sea: A Bird's-eye View* will directly support the Cornell Lab's projects, such as children's educational and community programs.

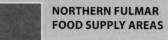

NORTHERN FULMAR
FOOD SUPPLY AREAS

NORTHERN FULMAR
BREEDING AREAS

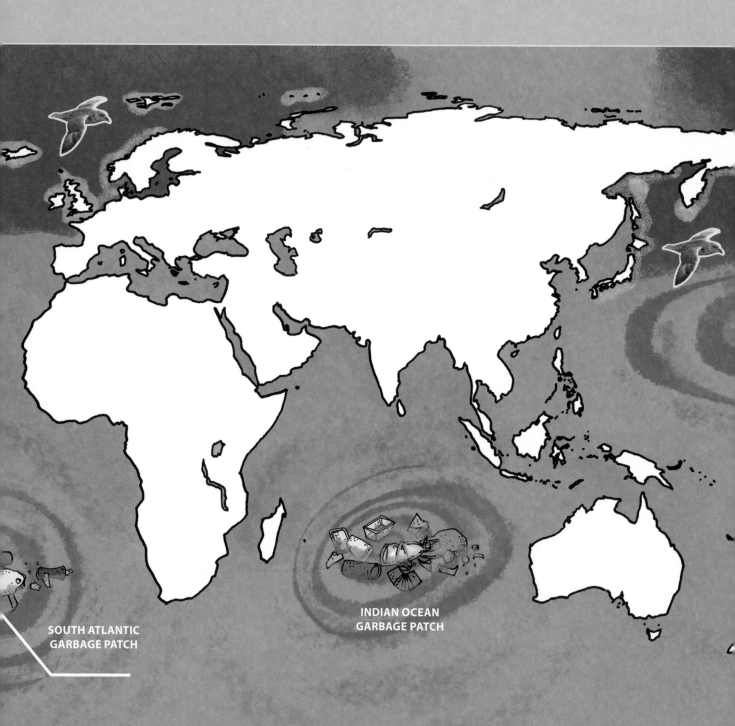

SOUTH ATLANTIC
GARBAGE PATCH

INDIAN OCEAN
GARBAGE PATCH